Date 2/1/12

J 599.276 NIC
Nichols, Catherine.
Tricky opossums /

GROSS-OUT DEFENSES

Tricky
OPOSSUMS

by Catherine Nichols

Consultant: Gabrielle Sachs
Zoo Educator

BEARPORT
PUBLISHING

NEW YORK, NEW YORK

Credits

Cover, © Mark Hamblin; TOC-L, © John Bell/Shutterstock; TOC-R, © MBurnham/Istockphoto; 4-5, © Steve Maslowski/Maslowski Productions; 6, © David Kuhn/Dwight Kuhn Photography; 7, © Konrad Wothe/Minden Pictures; 8, © Lynda Richardson/Corbis; 9, © Jeffrey Lepore/Photo Researchers, Inc.; 10, © Steve Maslowski/Maslowski Productions; 11, © Waverley Traylor/Dismal Swamp Photography; 12, © Alan Gleichman/Shutterstock; 13, © Thomas Kitchin & Victoria Hurst; 14, © David Liebman Photography; 15, © Frank Lukasseck/Corbis; 16, © Gary Meszaros/ Photo Researchers, Inc.; 17, © Martin Rugner/Superstock; 18-19, © R. Wittek/ArcoImages/Peter Arnold, Inc.; 20, © Len Rue Jr./Leonard Rue Enterprises, Inc.; 21, © Waverley Traylor/Dismal Swamp Photography; 22, © Ed Reschke/Peter Arnold Inc.; 23TL, © Alan Gleichman/Shutterstock; 23TR, © William Leaman/Alamy; 23BL, © Gary Meszaros/Photo Researchers, Inc.; 23BR, © Martin Rugner/Superstock.

Publisher: Kenn Goin
Senior Editor: Lisa Wiseman
Creative Director: Spencer Brinker
Design: Becky Munich
Photo Researcher: Amy Dunleavy

Library of Congress Cataloging-in-Publication Data
Nichols, Catherine.
  Tricky opossums / by Catherine Nichols.
      p. cm. — (Gross-out defenses)
  Includes bibliographical references and index.
  ISBN-13: 978-1-59716-718-5 (library binding)
  ISBN-10: 1-59716-718-5 (library binding)
  1. Opossums—Juvenile literature. 2. Animal defenses—Juvenile literature. I. Title.

  QL737.M34N53 2009
  599.2'76—dc22
                                    2008005942

For more information, write to Bearport Publishing Company, Inc., 101 Fifth Avenue, Suite 6R, New York, New York 10003. Printed in the United States of America in North Mankato, Minnesota.

052010
042910CG

10 9 8 7 6 5 4 3

Contents

In Trouble

The opossum waddled into the backyard.

It didn't see the dog lying under a tree.

The dog, however, spotted the opossum.

It got up and rushed toward the small animal.

The scared opossum flopped on its side.

It didn't move, not even when the dog sniffed it.

Was the opossum dead?

No, it was just pretending.

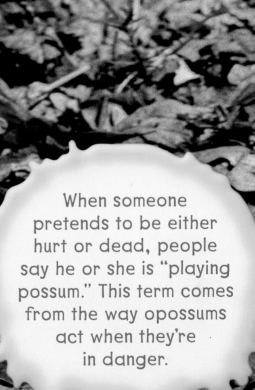

When someone pretends to be either hurt or dead, people say he or she is "playing possum." This term comes from the way opossums act when they're in danger.

Acting Tough

When facing an **enemy**, an opossum doesn't always play dead right away.

Often it climbs the nearest tree or fence to escape.

If the opossum can't get away, it tries to scare off its enemy.

It snarls and shows its 50 sharp teeth.

An opossum may also hiss, growl, and screech to make itself seem scary.

Great horned owls, dogs, foxes, and coyotes are some of the animals that like to eat opossums.

Playing Dead

When all other tricks fail, an opossum will fall over on its side.

Its curled-up body becomes stiff and its tongue hangs out of its mouth.

The opossum's breathing also begins to slow down.

It looks like it's dead!

The animal can stay this way for up to four hours.

While playing dead, an opossum might poop, blow bubbles of drool out of its nose, or squirt out a smelly, green liquid from its backside. Phew! What kind of animal would want to eat something so gross?

Time to Wake Up

An opossum plays dead until its enemy gives up and goes away.

Even when poked, shaken, or bitten, the opossum won't move.

After a while, it wiggles its ears to listen for sounds.

If all seems quiet, the opossum picks up its head and looks around.

At the first sign of danger, the opossum flops over again.

An opossum has no control over pretending to be dead. When it's scared, its body stiffens on its own, making the animal look dead. Although the opossum can't move, it still knows what's going on around it.

A Safe Home

During the day, the opossum doesn't worry about its enemies too much.

It stays safe in its home, called a **den**.

A den may be in a tree, under a porch, or in a rock pile.

Sometimes opossums even use dens left by other animals.

Inside the dens they make cozy nests out of grass and leaves.

den

Opossums leave their dens at night to search for food. Using their sharp sense of smell, they hunt snakes, insects, birds, frogs, and mice. They also eat fruit, nuts, dead animals, and smelly garbage.

Teeny-Tiny Babies

Mother opossums use their dens to have babies, called joeys.

They can give birth to up to 20 joeys in one **litter**.

The babies are born blind and furless.

Each joey is very tiny—about the size of a honeybee.

joeys

Baby opossums are born with teeny-tiny tails. As they get older, their tails grow very long—about 9 to 20 inches (23 to 51 cm). Opossums' tails are strong enough to help them grasp things and keep their balance while climbing tree branches.

A Place to Grow Big

After the tiny babies are born, they crawl into a pouch on their mother's stomach.

Since they can't see, they need help finding the pouch.

Their mother licks the fur on her stomach.

The little ones follow the path of damp fur to the pouch.

Once inside, the joeys drink their mother's milk.

joeys

Opossums are **marsupials**. Most marsupials, such as kangaroos, live in Australia. The opossum is the only marsupial that is found in North America.

kangaroo

pouch

Hanging On

After eight weeks, each baby is about the size of a mouse.

The babies are too big to all fit inside the pouch now.

However, they're still too young to live on their own.

So the joeys climb onto their mother's back.

She gives her babies a piggyback ride as she looks for food.

If a young opossum falls off its mother's back, it makes sneezing noises. This sound helps the mother opossum find her lost joey.

19

Staying Safe

When an opossum is about five months old, it's ready to live on its own.

Its mother has taught it how to find food and make a nest.

It's also ready to protect itself.

If one of its enemies comes by, the young opossum knows just how to fool it.

Opossums do not have long lives. Most live for only about two years in the wild.

Another Tricky Defense

Like the opossum, the hognose snake acts dead to fool its enemies. If the snake can't scare an enemy away, it will flip over and pretend to be dead. Then it lets out a stinky smell. Phew! Sometimes drops of blood drip from the snake's open mouth. If the snake has just eaten, it will spit up its last meal. Yuck! The snake doesn't move until its enemy leaves. Then it rolls over on its belly and slithers away.

Glossary

den (DEN) a home where an opossum rests, hides from enemies, and has babies

enemy (EN-uh-mee) an animal that hunts another animal for food

litter (LIT-ur) a group of babies born at the same time that have the same mother

marsupials (mar-SOO-pee-uhlz) a group of animals, which includes opossums and kangaroos, that carry their babies in pouches on their stomachs

Index

Read More

Walker, Sally M. *Opossum at Sycamore Road*. Norwalk, CT: Soundprints (1997).

Webster, Christine. *Opossums*. New York: Weigl Publishers (2007).

Whitehouse, Patricia. *Opossums*. Chicago: Heinemann Library (2002).

Learn More Online

To learn more about opossums, visit
www.bearportpublishing.com/GrossOutDefenses

About the Author

Catherine Nichols has written many books for children, including several on animals. She lives in upstate New York with her dog and two cats.